EAT UGLY

and other simple tips to improve your health

Dr. Aaron McMichael

Copyright © 2024 Aaron McMichael

All rights reserved

No part of this book may be reproduced, or stored in a retrieval system, or transmitted in any form or by any means, electronic, mechanical, photocopying, recording, or otherwise, without express written permission of the publisher.

ISBN: 9798323480517

Cover design and illustrations by: Aaron McMichael

Library of Congress Control Number: 2018675309

Printed in the United States of America

To my family, one of the healthiest and most loving I know.

CONTENTS

Introduction	vi
Eat Well	3
Move It	29
Perfect Posture	47
Stress Less	65
Rest Best	83
Care About Health	99
Your Environment	123
Take Action	145
About the Author	147

INTRODUCTION

Being healthy has become needlessly complicated.

It shouldn't require a PhD in nutrition, a personal trainer, and a team of medical specialists performing endless testing and prescribing lists of medications to live a long, healthy life. There are those that benefit from this unnecessary complication, but it is rarely the patient.

Evidence is clearer than ever that **you** have the greatest control over your health. You have more control than your genes or your doctor. The biggest impact on your health is your lifestyle. Not the medication you take or the medical intervention you experience.

Don't blame your genes. The major chronic issues affecting many Americans are lifestyle related. Your habits are the problem. But it's not all your fault. Americans are bombarded almost constantly with marketing messages that encourage them to make horrible choices and there are few strong voices proclaiming these choices lead to early disease and death.

Enough doom and gloom. Knowing that you control your health is uplifting and empowering. Your genetics don't resign you to a life of suffering. You determine your health outcomes. You can actually control your genes. The field of epigenetics is involved with how our habits and environment change the expression of our genes. We have so much more to learn about this, but here is the point: if you want a longer, healthier life, you can make it happen. That's what this book is for.

This book is not a long, academic read of research full of medical speak. Years ago, I read Michael Pollan's wonderful book called *Food Rules*. I recommend it for those who would like more simple guidance for better eating choices. The book is simple and straightforward with memorable ways to make better choices when buying food and sitting down to eat.

Like *Food Rules*, this book is written to give you a guide with simple memorable rules or tips to make better choices with not just eating, but other important health habits. These suggestions are supported by research, work with patients over years of practice, and a healthy dose of common sense. Each rule could be turned into its own book. However, the point is to provide simple ideas with a brief explanation. Some are so straightforward they require almost no explanation. Others may include a story or illustration to make the point.

Some may sound familiar with a bit of a twist while others are totally new. There is a little redundancy with a few of these rules. You don't have to be perfect with all of them. Remember the ones that stick and stick to them.

You may not be ready for certain rules or need to check with your provider first (intense exercise activity). Start with what you can and work up from there. And applaud yourself along the way. Focus on what you are doing well to encourage yourself to do more. Keep applauding yourself along the way. You will be healthier with each step you take.

The rules in this book are organized into 7 categories to provide a comprehensive foundation of good habits: eating, activity, posture, stress, sleep, healthcare, and your environment.

Picture all of these habits as potential stress on your body or a potential boost to your health. Poor habits all end up in the same pile weighing you down and degrading your health. Our amazingly adaptive bodies can handle a reasonable level of stress, but for many this pile is too big. Every good habit takes a stressor out of that pile to reduce the total amount of stress on your body. Fewer stressors reduce negative stress responses and trigger less inflammation throughout your body. Every bit helps. That is why a variety of healthy habits can improve the same health problem. They can all reduce barriers to healing and let the body do what it is programmed to do: be healthy.

As you start improving your habits, try to include a rule from each section. Once you have done that, keep building. If you can follow even half of the rules in each section fairly consistently, you are well on your way to better health.

There may be a hurdle you need to address before you can follow a rule. It could be a person in your life that pushes you to make poor choices. It could be a place or situation. Recognize what it is and address it. Find help to address it if needed. You can do this. You can and will be healthier.

"Keep your vitality. A life without health is like a river without water."

MAXIME LAGACE

EAT WELL

Healthy eating is the foundation of a healthy life, yet it is the biggest stumbling block for most Americans. You could follow every other healthy habit, but if your eating is poor your health will be poor.

We eat so differently than our ancestors did only generations ago, but processed food manufacturers and their paid experts want us to believe it does not matter. It matters. I have yet to find a patient that can get away with bad eating habits. They may appear to be temporarily invincible, but it is only a matter of time before their health goes downhill.

Health is not just how you look or feel. Skinny does not equal health. Feeling ok on medication does not equal health. You should look and feel healthy but do not let this trick you into thinking it automatically makes you healthy. The body has a great ability to adapt to stressors but only until it cannot adapt anymore.

If you are eating junk, it is impairing your health and it will cause problems eventually. Eat better and you will be better.

1. Eat Real Food.

While you can find a diet "expert" to proclaim the virtues of any crazy diet imaginable, there is one thing that anyone with integrity can agree on: eat less processed food. What should we eat? Real food. Real whole food. Food our ancestors have eaten for ages and our bodies recognize.

Processed food has gone through a type of manufacturing to increase its ability to sell, not its healthfulness. Usually this means it can sit longer on a shelf to avoid waste or it can be made much cheaper than other options. Those are both good for business but rarely good for our health, and food companies have figured out how to trick us into thinking their food-like substance is food.

If a substance is pretending to be real food, you are best avoiding it. Think of American cheese product, margarine or fake butter spreads, imitation maple syrup, whipped topping, fruit drink, and artificial sugars. Making them appear to be the real product usually requires heavy processing (that destroys nutrients) and the addition of chemical flavors, texturizers, preservatives, colors, etc.

Unless you have a specific allergy, just eat the least processed version you can find of real food: meat, veggies, fruit, nuts, seeds, dairy, oils, etc.

2. You Can't Outrun A Bad Diet.

Exercise does not give you an excuse to eat junk. Sure, increased activity will allow your body to tolerate more sugary carbs as it burns them faster. But do not kid yourself into thinking you can exercise your way out of a bad diet.

A patient from years ago comes to mind that injured his neck and ruptured a disc in his spine. He had constant severe pain through the neck and arm and went through spinal disc surgery. He felt better after the surgery, but soon ruptured the neighboring disc and his severe arm and neck pain returned. He did not want surgery again, so he went about staying active with exercise and was otherwise healthier than average.

This patient eventually showed up at our clinic for help with his eating habits expecting to lose a few extra pounds. Within three weeks of eating MUCH better, his constant neck and arm pain from the disc injury were gone. He was doing great at exercise, but his diet was increasing his inflammation and pain. Once he ate better, his inflammation reduced and his disc injury no longer caused him pain. We have seen plenty of intense exercisers that cannot achieve their health goals until they eat better.

There is more to exercise than burning calories. Exercise without healthy eating will only take you so far.

3. An *Organic* Apple A Day Keeps The Doctor Away.

Or a chemical-free apple a day keeps the doctor away. Like most produce, the apple in the grocery store today is not what it once was. It does not pack the same nutritional punch.

Organic is not just about avoiding chemicals that increase your risk of health issues. Plants grown without these chemicals are also higher in nutrients – vitamins, minerals, and other plant compounds that have health benefits for us. A scientific analysis of organic vs conventional versions makes it look almost like analyzing different plants.

Think about a plant that does not have to fight off challenges because it is coddled with chemicals and other modern farming techniques. Sure, it grows big and beautiful, but without challenges it does not have a chance to flex its muscles and develop strength. The plant makes fewer natural compounds inside to repel bugs and repair damage. Its roots do not have to reach deep for water (reaching more minerals at the same time) because of surface irrigation. It does not get a smorgasbord of nutrients from natural compost. It only gets the big three from chemical fertilizers: nitrogen, phosphorus, and potassium. It is just a pretty façade without the same nutrition.

To be continued…

4. Eat Ugly.

That ugly apple grown without chemical inputs has fought and survived. Maybe it has a scar or blemish, but if only you could see the inner beauty which is a bounty of nutrients! That fight has increased the apple's production and concentration of nutrients. These nutrients help defend that apple but also help improve our health.

An apple that looks perfect with no blemish could be ok or could be all looks. Do not avoid the ugly ones because odds are they are better for you. It does not have to be certified organic but try to limit your consumption of produce grown in a fog of chemicals.

5.   Thicker Peel, Fewer Chemicals.

We know which produce contains the most pesticides and herbicide chemicals. Studies on the average chemical content inside fruits and veggies grown in the United States have been performed regularly for years now with consistent results. Produce with thick inedible peels tend to be low in chemical residues while those with thin edible peels tend to have the highest concentration of chemicals in their flesh.

Thick peels are likely to help for two reasons: 1. They provide a better defense for the plant so fewer chemical sprays are needed to kill pests. 2. They provide a better defense against chemical sprays that are used.

These studies have been done with washed and peeled produce, testing only the edible inside. Washing and peeling may help but it will not eliminate the chemicals.

Those thick-peeled, low chemical produce are items like pineapples, avocados, and onions. The thin-peeled high chemical produce are items like apples, strawberries, and peaches.

Consider choosing organic versions for produce containing the highest chemical load or shift to consuming more produce with a lower chemical load to reduce your chemical intake. For more information check out the EWG's Dirty Dozen list.

6. Eating In Moderation Produces Moderate Health.

Do you want moderate health? Is your goal to be as healthy as the average American? That is a rather low bar. When we trick ourselves to believe "everything in moderation," we give ourselves an excuse to eat any junky food-like substance as long as we don't gorge on it.

How about aiming higher? Perfection is not necessary to be healthy, but moderation will only take you so far. You can do better. Eat well to be well.

7. Water Is Wonderful.

There is nothing better you can put in your body. We are made to drink water. Lots of water, every day. Sports drinks are not an improvement on water. Vitamin waters are not an improvement on water. Juices are not an improvement on water. Give your body what it wants and needs to function its best: water.

If you have fooled your body too long into not enjoying water, add a slice of lemon (not lemon flavoring).

8. It's Not A Treat If You Eat It All The Time.

Maybe you deserve a treat. But you do not deserve a treat for every meal. And you do not deserve a treat every day unless your treat is a fun or healthy activity.

You do not have to eat perfectly to be healthy, but you do have to eat well most of the time. Save the snack or dessert treats for special occasions or events. Cut the sweets and baked goods and find better ways to reward yourself.

9. Eat Bugs To Beat Bugs.

I am not referring to insects, though you may eat those if you want. This is about healthy microbes. Every culture seems to have included a fermented food in their diet. Germans eat sauerkraut. Koreans eat kimchi. French eat stinky cheeses. All around the world are cultures that ferment food by allowing microbes in the environment to eat their sugars and convert the sugars into acids. This helps naturally preserve the food so it can stay edible without refrigeration. It is also like a form of predigestion that makes the food easier for us to digest and makes the nutrients more available.

And healthy microbes come along for the ride when we eat these foods (if they have not been pasteurized). The research on our microbiome is growing as scientists are becoming more aware of the importance of the bugs in us and on us.

Healthy microbes benefit our immune system, digestive system, and mood among other things. We have much more to learn but know enough to include them regularly in our diet with fermented foods or probiotics.

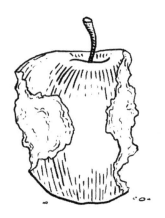

10. Don't Eat Sometimes.

In our modern convenient world, we could eat food every minute we are awake and never feel a tinge of hunger. Most of us do not eat constantly, but we do eat often.

How does this modern way of eating multiple meals and snacks every day compare to our ancestors? It was not that many thousands of years ago that we were lucky to eat one good meal each day. Go back far enough and we were more likely to experience cycles of relative feast and famine.

Before reliable food preservation, we ate our fill when food was available. And then it was not available, so we would go hungry for a bit. This fluctuated with hunting success and with the seasons of the year. We packed on the pounds during times of abundance to survive cooler winters of scarcity.

The idea of increasing time between meals with no nutrient intake is called intermittent fasting and is catching on. It seems to be what our bodies expect to be their best so it is a good idea to incorporate it into your routine. Start by finishing eating earlier in the evening, then work on starting to eat later in the day. Some like to pick a day each week to fast. There are many ways to do it and plenty of resources available that provide more information. Give it a try. It is ok to feel hungry.

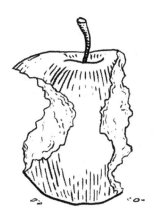

11. Eat With Others.

Eating meals with others is beneficial in many ways. Picture a time when you were eating alone, maybe not even sitting down to enjoy the meal. Mindlessly scarfing it down. What were you eating? Probably nothing healthy.

Communal meals are the best meals for us. We slow down and take more time to digest and enjoy the meal and those we share it with.

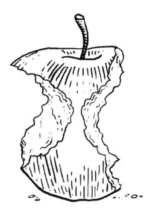

12. Eat Real Whole Food Or Whole Food Supplements.

Nearly every health care provider agrees that real whole foods provide the best nutrition. But what type of supplements provide the best nutrition when our diet is inadequate? Whole food supplements. In other words, supplements made from concentrating whole foods (veggies, fruits, herbs, organ meats, bone, etc.).

Most vitamins on the store shelves are synthesized chemicals made as cheaply and efficiently as possible. There is a place for these supplements, but they are nothing like the nutrients found in a food that come as a complex. An average multivitamin contains a dozen selected synthetic vitamins. Compare that to an apple with over 200 known nutrients including vitamins, minerals, cofactors, phytochemicals, etc.

The list of nutrients in an apple grows every year. Not because apples are becoming more nutritious, but because we learn about more nutrients visible with improved technology. That is why, as a whole food, an apple can provide more nutrition than a supplement. And a supplement carefully made by concentrating the nutrients in the apple (not cooking them away) can provide more nutrition than a synthetic combination created in a lab.

MOVE IT

Like everyone else, you know exercise is good for you. Here are helpful rules to keep in mind.

13. Move It Or Lose It.

Exercise and movement are more than just burning calories to maintain a healthy weight. Your body is dependent on motion to be healthy. Your muscles and ligaments need to stretch and contract regularly. Your joints need to move through their full ranges of motion to stay lubricated and free and minimize the development of arthritis. Your bones need to move against weight and gravity to encourage them to build or maintain strength. Your brain and nerves need to be fired regularly to signal motion throughout the body and control your body's position and balance. And that is just the neuromusculoskeletal system. There is also the cardiovascular system, respiratory system, digestive system…they all benefit from motion.

As soon as you retire to a chair you are retiring to the degradation of health. Sometimes a very fast degradation of health. So keep moving.

14. Go Slow A Long Time, Lift Heavy Stuff Regularly, Speed Occasionally.

This is your simple blueprint for healthy activity.

Go slow a long time – spend three or more hours each week taking long, leisurely walks, bikes, swims, etc.

Lift heavy stuff regularly – spend 20-60 minutes per week lifting heavy stuff or doing something to challenge your strength.

Speed occasionally – perform brief sprints or high intensity activity for a few minutes once per week.

15. Walking A Mile Makes You Smile.

If there is one activity that everyone should/must do, it is walking. We are walking machines. Walking regularly has great health benefits and is about the easiest, no-cost exercise you can do. No training required. No special equipment needed. You can do it almost anywhere. Your body craves it.

Walking is not just great for you physically, it is also very beneficial mentally. It brings emotional balance and elevates your mood. I will accept a walk on the treadmill, but you really boost the benefits by walking outside. You can max it out by walking deeper in nature away from signs of civilization (more on that later).

16. Sweat Regularly.

Regular low intensity activity like walking is great, but make sure you also include activity intense enough to make you sweat or start breathing harder. This does not need to be nearly as long as your walking or other low intensity activity, but it should be a regular part of your routine to challenge your body to increase strength and stamina.

17. Hit Your Limit On Limited Occasions.

Make sure you have aced the previous two rules before you attempt this one. Everyone should hit their limit but not everyone is ready for it. HIT or high intensity training is a term for this. Exercising very hard to the point of exhaustion for only a brief period. This is exercising so intensely that you cannot do it for more than several minutes total.

Sprinting, cycling, and swimming are common ways to do this. Take your pick. Once you are comfortable with one of these activities at a moderate level, try a burst of speed going close to your max for maybe half a minute. Then settle down to any easy walk, peddle, or paddle again to rest a bit. A cycle or two of this intense activity may be enough for your first attempt. Eventually you can work toward several cycles, usually no more than 30 seconds long with a minute of low activity in between.

This intense activity creates great health benefits in a very short exercise time.

18. Bend, Don't Break.

Flexibility often gets overlooked in favor of building strength, but it is just as important. Our ability to flex and bend through our joints and soft tissues improves our ability to be active and helps reduce the risk of injury. Don't be stiff and brittle. Be fluid and flexible.

19. Challenge Your Balance To Avoid Falls.

Balance can be exercised and improved just like strength and flexibility. Do not wait until it gets bad either. Start now to avoid the risk of falls and injuries in the future. If you cannot balance on one foot with your eyes closed for 30 seconds, you have work to do.

Maintaining balance requires your brain and nerve sensors around your body to work in synch. Your brain must read signals about where your body parts are and where they are moving to. Then it needs to send signals to your muscles so your body can respond and maintain balance.

Think about those nerves carrying the signals to and from the brain. You do not want that information travelling on an infrequently used little dirt path. You want a ten-lane superhighway. You want the nerve autobahn in your body.

How? Use it. Every time you move in a way that challenges your balance, you work those nerve pathways. The more they work, the more they transform from a dirt path to a racetrack. Do anything that challenges your balance. Start small if needed. Stand on a towel and work toward standing on a thick pillow. Stand on one foot, hop on one foot, side plank. Then try these with your eyes closed.

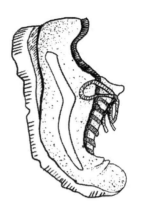

20. Don't Exercise, Have Active Fun.

If you do not like exercise, then do not exercise. Just have fun being active instead. Play sports with friends. Go canoeing or kayaking. Take the family skating or skiing. Go on a nature hike. Turn on your favorite music and get dancing. Find an activity you enjoy, and you are more likely to make it part of your life. The best activity is the one you will do regularly.

PERFECT POSTURE

Hunching over is not just for old people anymore. Look around in public. Bad posture is for everyone these days. Technology is part of the problem, but nothing prevents you from doing better.

Posture is an underrated contributor to health. Studies have demonstrated a link to bad posture and lower life expectancy. It is time to take posture seriously and straighten up!

21. Stand Strong, Live Long.

Posture is key for a well-functioning body. When you are standing, do you stand strong? Or do you look weak and hunched over? It takes a little effort to stand with good posture but it is worth it. You look better and you feel better. Better posture immediately helps your mood and improves your health in more ways than one.

22. Head Back, Thumbs Forward.

Here are two body parts to help you think about how to improve your posture. The main one is your head. Your head should be over top of your shoulders, not in front of them. That means when looking at you from the side, your ear should line up with your shoulder or arm. No more head slouched forward, pulling on your neck and back. This posture adds pounds of stress to your neck and upper back, often leading to discomfort and arthritis with time.

Next look at your arms. Are your shoulders curled in hiding your chest? Look at where your thumbs are pointing as your arms hang to the side. Do not let them point to each other. Move your shoulders back to where they belong and turn them out so the thumbs naturally point forward.

23. Spend More Time On Your Feet Than Your Bottom.

Maybe you have heard "sitting is the new smoking." With modern office jobs, we get stuck sitting all day long. Then we go home and...sit.

Get off your buns. We are made to move and stand, not sit all day. As common as poor posture is when we stand, it is often worse when we sit. Some people have the posture of a blob when they sit. So stop sitting so much. Almost everything you do sitting, you can also do standing. Raise your workspace if needed or find a counter or higher surface to work on at times.

24. Pull Up The String Attached To Your Head.

If you tell people to straighten up, some turn into an overexaggerated soldier with their head crammed back and chest puffed out. That is not a natural posture that will work for you so here is another way to think about moving into a correct posture.

Picture a string attached to the very top of your head and imagine someone pulling it straight up. Allow your upper body to lift with the string and you will find your body moving closer to an optimal position.

25. Don't Bow To Technology.

Modern technology is a big hurdle to good posture. When was the last time you saw someone looking at their phone with good posture? As soon as the phone is in hand, then their head bows down to look at it.

You have two options to fix this (that do not include throwing the phone out): 1. Raise the phone up in front of you to avoid the tendency to hunch over it. 2. Talk without looking at it so you are not tempted into poor posture.

Working at computers similarly sucks us in to hunch mode, so keep your monitor up at a good level and remind yourself to stay upright.

26. Bend With A Twist And Injure A Disc.

Bending forward increases stress on the discs in your spine. Twisting also increases stress on the discs in your spine. Bending down and twisting to the side at the same time increases stress on your discs even more. Now lift something off the ground once you are down there and you are maximizing the stress on your spinal discs. Do it enough and you could cause a disc injury.

To reduce your risk of injury from bad posture, move your feet! Don't plant your feet in one spot, bending and reaching all over. Move those feet around to place your body in the best position.

Consider how you sweep, rake, or vacuum. Are you standing in one spot and reaching all over, or are your feet doing the work to get you where you need to be? Think about dancing with that vacuum if you must. It is all about the footwork.

27. Stand Like Royalty.

Imagine a king or queen standing in front of their subjects. Are they hunched over or standing tall and proud? You do not have to be royalty to stand like one. Just don't stick your nose too high in the air.

28. Head To The Wall.

Here is one last method to get your head in the right position. Stand with your back against the wall. Now slide your head back until it touches the wall. That is where it should be. If you have a chronically hunched back you may not be able to get there, but most of us should.

STRESS LESS

There is more understanding today of the negative effects of stress on our health. That includes both mental and physical health.

Our bodies are made to handle short term stresses, but today's world of ongoing daily stresses hammers our health. Think of this stressful situation from generations ago. You are out in the wild and end up perilously close to a bear. Your body gears up the cardiorespiratory and musculoskeletal systems to run away in an all-out effort. It also heightens your senses. Full steam to the engines! At the same time, it shuts down temporarily unimportant functions like digestion. This adaptive response to an environmental stress gives you the best chance of survival. And this episode is usually over in minutes whether you survive or not.

Compare that to modern stressors. They may start with dealing with the kids, then work, then a problem with lunch, then after-work activities, family issues, financial problems, etc. These repeated daily stresses are much harder on the body and result in more health problems over time.

We can't get rid of every stress in our life, but we can reduce them and find ways to moderate others.

29. Nature Is Best To Melt Away Stress.

We are made to be in nature. The further we go from nature, the more problems we have. Go out and experience nature as deeply and as often as you can.

Japanese studies on "forest bathing" (not taking a bath in the forest, just immersing yourself in nature) have found immediate and significant benefits to spending time in nature. Stress hormones measurably reduce after a walk in the woods compared to those who take a walk through the city.

Deeper is better. Go somewhere with no signs of civilization if possible.

If you cannot get away from civilization, go where you can minimize it, like a park.

If you cannot get outside, look outside at nature.

And if you do not have a window or a view of nature, look at a picture of nature. Even that helps reduce stress.

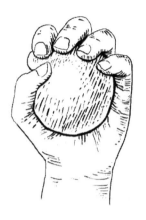

30. Deep Breaths De-Stress.

Breathing deeply and slowly have an almost magical effect on our body. Make them deep belly breaths by ensuring your belly is moving in and out with each deep breath as your major diaphragm muscle does the work. You do not want your breathing to be shallow upper body chest breathing with smaller muscles. If the movement is all through your chest and shoulders, refocus on breathing with your belly.

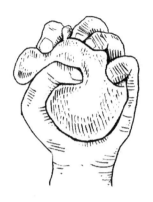

31. Dirty Hands, Clear Mind.

Digging your hands into real soil improves mood balance. It may be the healthy microbes we encounter in soil that cause this effect. It may be something else about being active in nature. Regardless, dig in the dirt and plant something with your hands. If you don't have a yard, use a pot.

32. Follow Your Purpose.

Your purpose does not have to be earth shattering but it must exist. A study of regions with populations commonly living to 100+ years found that purpose was one of the common findings in those living a long healthy life. Some continued working in fulfilling jobs well into their 90s. Others found a purpose in helping their community. If you have no reason to exist, how long will you keep going? Find your purpose and pursue it.

33. Do Nothing Daily.

Everyone needs a break sometimes. Even if it is just five minutes a day, take quiet time for yourself to relax and de-stress.

34. Laugh A Little, Live A Lot.

Maybe laughter is the best medicine. Surround yourself with those that bring you joy and know how to give you a good hearty laugh.

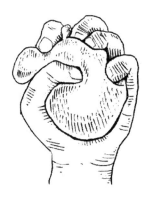

35. Appreciate Others To Improve Yourself.

Gifting something to others has been shown to emotionally benefit the giver as much as the receiver. Think about everyone in your life and all the little and big things they have done and continue to do for you and others. Thank them and genuinely appreciate them.

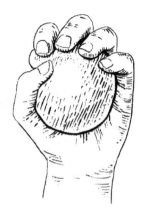

36. Give Yourself A Break.

You are not perfect. No one is. It is ok. Do your best and forgive yourself for making mistakes. Focus on doing better next time.

REST BEST

Sleep provides the opportunity for your body to recover from the day's activity.

Instead of going through a long list of benefits from good sleep, just think about the effects on your brain alone. Sleep is vital to brain function. When sleeping, your brain goes to work responding to that day's input and building for the next day. Sleeping is like parking your brain in the garage each night for a tune up. Without a healthy brain to control the processes occurring every second in your body, your health goes downhill fast. Do your brain and entire body a favor and give it the rest it needs.

37. Sleep 7 Hours Plus And See Less Fuss.

Studies indicate seven hours of solid sleep is the minimum needed for most everyone. Even those who think they do well with less have been shown to underperform when tested. Some need nine or more hours. Age, activity, and injury all factor into our need for sleep.

Less than seven hours of sleep causes immediate effects on memory, mood, blood sugar, concentration, immune system function, blood pressure, and balance among other things. Do not cut yourself short.

38. Sleep Back Or Side, Beds Aren't To Ride.

Stop sleeping on your stomach. It places more stress on your back and neck, and is likely to lead to problems at some point. Sleep on your back or side for the best position.

39. Pillow Too Thick Or Pillow Too Flat, Makes A Neck Stiff Or Makes A Sore Back.

There is no magic number of pillows or type of filling to use. There is an ideal thickness though. Your pillow or pillows should be thick enough to keep your head straight in a neutral position. This is thinner for back sleepers and thicker for side sleepers.

40. Don't Be Afraid Of The Dark.

Minimize the light in your room for more restful sleep. The darker the better to avoid light which reduces melatonin production and interferes with proper rest. Even dim light can affect melatonin, so save the night light for the hall.

41. Celebrate Siesta.

Some cultures know how to nap. Even a short break to rest in the afternoon can be good for the mind and body.

42.   Sleep To Heal.

Sleep time is healing time. While the body gets a break from the day's activity, it goes into repair mode to work on what you threw at it that day. Studies on wound healing have demonstrated significantly slower healing when sleep is inadequate. The more trauma your body is recovering from, the more sleep it needs.

43.   Sleep To Perform.

Sleep and rest are just as important as exercise when it comes to performance. Make healthy sleep part of your exercise routine.

CARE ABOUT HEALTH

You have probably heard the statistics. The United States provides some of the most advanced health care in the world, but we spend more than every other country and end up nowhere near the top of the list for best outcomes. We are doing something wrong.

Part of what we are doing wrong is our lifestyle, which is what this book is for! The other part is the care we use to address our health challenges, which this section is for...

44. Deal With The Small Stuff To Avoid The Big Stuff.

"An ounce of prevention is worth a pound of cure," right? Early treatment is also worth far more than delayed treatment. The earlier you can address a health problem the easier it is to get under control. Early is better than late treatment, and prevention is even better.

A prediabetic has a much better chance than a diabetic of controlling blood sugar and avoiding the harmful effects of diabetes. Eating well before being diagnosed as prediabetic is even better.

A new muscle strain is much easier and faster to improve than a chronic strain injury that has been going on for years. For example, take care of a foot problem before it makes you walk funny, aggravating your knees, hips, or back.

Your body can tolerate a lot but that does not mean it should. Take care of yourself before problems become more chronic and complex.

45. Healing Starts With You.

If you expect to be a passive spectator with your doctor or provider taking all the action to improve your health, good luck. Your chance of living a healthy life is low. You may feel reasonably well for a while, but you will not stay healthy without taking your own action to improve your habits.

46. Arthritis Is Caused By Old Injuries Not Old Age, But Acting Younger Helps Stop It.

Almost everyone experiences arthritis in life, yet it is often misunderstood even by medical providers. Age does not cause arthritis. Osteoarthritis, also known as degenerative arthritis, develops when there is too much stress and strain on a joint or surrounding tissues. This develops from a sudden injury or ongoing stress like that caused by poor posture day after day. Age just gives old injuries and poor habits a chance to create arthritis.

The body responds to extra stress on joints by making the surrounding soft tissue more solid and bone-like to absorb the stress. Over time this looks like the bone is growing and forming bone spurs or rough pointy edges. Let this process go on long enough and you experience more than just stiffness. If can start to pinch on nerves, causing sharper pains and numbness or tingling.

The key to slowing or stopping this degenerative process is healthy movement of the joints and soft tissues. Lack of movement accelerates arthritis and healthy movement slows arthritis. Stay active and incorporate manual treatments like chiropractic adjusting and physiotherapies to reduce stress on the area and keep those joints moving.

47. Avoid A Cure That's Worse Than The Disease.

Interventions too often do not weigh benefit and harm for each patient. The risk-benefit ratio is different for each patient based on their health and habits. Do not consider an intervention until you understand both positive and negative outcomes to determine if it is best for you.

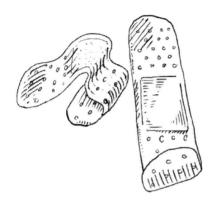

48. Start Conservative To Avoid Invasive.

The highest risk, most invasive treatments are rarely needed yet data tells us they are far overused. More is not always better. In this case, more is worse.

Back surgery is a good example. Back surgeons agree that back surgery is performed more often than necessary. Most back pain and even spinal disc injuries do not require back surgery. Long-range studies show even those surgeries that go well often have the same results when compared to those who avoided surgery after a couple years. Are there cases where the risk of surgery makes sense for the injury? Yes. But most cases respond well to conservative drug-free treatment like chiropractic adjusting, therapeutic exercise, acupuncture, etc.

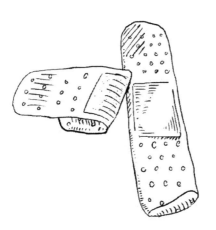

49. Don't Ask An Electrician How To Fix Your Toilet.

Experts are knowledgeable about their expertise. Medical doctors are knowledgeable about medicine and surgeons are experts on surgery. Specialists know about their specialty. There is too much research being published every day for any provider type to keep up with all of it.

Yet, patients often ask medical providers about treatments that these physicians are unfamiliar with. When interested in other treatment, be sure to ask the provider who specializes in that treatment. Your medical provider may be able to help by suggesting the provider type you are considering where you can get more detailed information.

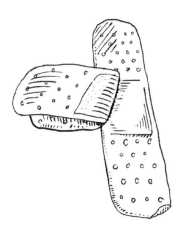

50. Being Healthy Is A Team Sport.

You will not be your healthiest alone. Your team should include not just health care providers, but others in your life that will help you be your best.

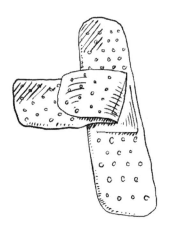

51. Change The Cause Not The Effect.

Too much focus is on reducing effects rather than addressing causes (in and beyond health care).

Growing masses of one crop year after year is efficient but creates an inviting feast for pests and depletes soil. Chemical sprays can control pests for a while and chemical fertilizers can keep crops growing. But these inputs create a lot of work, so GMOs are developed to mass spray rather than selective spraying crops. More sprays accelerate an arms race with resistant pests and superweeds that require more and stronger chemicals marketed as the solution…or some farmers recognize the root problem is that growing one crop dependent on massive synthetic inputs is not sustainable. They can avoid the arms race by switching to a rotational mixed crop (polyculture) farm benefiting from a variety of animals and plants supporting each other.

Similarly, poor health habits lead to pains that are often masked with over-the-counter pain relievers. Once these are not enough, prescription medication is used. As the problem worsens, injections are tried until relief no longer lasts and surgery is deployed starting the cycle over again with pain relievers…or improving habits and addressing pain with nondrug options to improve posture, mobility, and strength can reduce the risk of repeated episodes and dependence on medications.

Don't ignore the warning light. Fix the problem by addressing the cause.

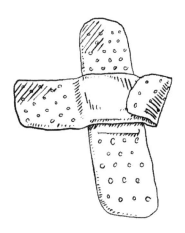

52. Overtesting Leads To Overtreating.

Modern medicine has developed an incredible arsenal of medical tests. These can provide great insight into diagnosing health conditions and determining the best treatment option. They can also lead to more and more testing and more and more sometimes unnecessary treatment.

Every test has a risk of being wrong. It could wrongly tell you there is a problem when there is not (false positive). It could wrongly tell you there is not problem when there is a problem (false negative).

Before undergoing testing, consider not just the risk of the test being performed but also the risk of inaccurate results. Even low risk tests can lead to problems if they are not accurate. Then consider how you will respond to recommendations based on the test. I have seen patients that will never follow through on a doctor's advice regardless of the test result. Is it worth bothering with the test in this case? Maybe it is if knowing the result at least provides some reassurance and eases the mind. Or if the test is for something life-threatening.

Medical tests can be very helpful, but make sure to keep the whole picture in mind.

53. An Emergency Room Is For Emergencies.

The emergency room is not the place for a comprehensive health examination. They have one job. They make sure your condition is stable and you will survive your health challenge. Once they have done their job, it is up to you to find a provider to address remaining health concerns.

Patients frequently are surprised at how little was done to address their non-lethal injury or complaint (or complaints 2, 3, 4, and 5). That is not their job. They make sure you will live and can make you more comfortable temporarily. Once the emergency is handled, you need to address your problem elsewhere.

54. More Chemicals Are Not The Answer.

Pharmaceuticals have their role in health care but these chemicals are not the answer to every health problem, and are not even the answer to most health problems. A lot of these problems are a result of our body's being bombarded by chemicals in our food and products. Why would consuming more chemicals be the answer?

YOUR ENVIRONMENT

Your environment has a bigger impact on your health than you may expect. And I am not just talking about the outdoor environment. This includes work and home. It includes where you play or pray. It includes the people you regularly encounter. All these parts of your environment nudge you into certain decisions affecting your health. Some you think about, and others you do not. Become aware of this and you can use it to your advantage.

55. You Are Your Environment.

If you lost your ability to sense your environment through sight, sound, and smell, where would your body think it is? Think about what your body comes in contact with on an average day. What goes in your body and what goes on your body?

Would your body think it is in the natural environment it is adapted to, encountering real food and items found commonly in nature? Or would your body think it is on an artificially lighted alien planet surrounded by a sea of chemicals in and around your body?

Your genetics have adapted to work well in a range of natural environments. Once you step far enough out of that range with food-like substances, chemical cleaners and cosmetics, and sunless indoor environments made of plastics and synthetics, your body must work hard to tolerate this environmental stress. The liver works with other organs to constantly clear wastes and chemicals from the body, but it does not have an unlimited capacity to do so.

Overloading on chemicals will harm your health. Reduce chemicals used in your house and chemicals in your foods to reduce the effect on your health.

56. Clean Is Good. Sanitized Is Bad.

Leave sanitization for the factories and facilities. Your home should be clean but not sanitized or sterile. There has been data for years now that shows kids growing up with animals (less clean environment) tend to be healthier with fewer allergies than those raised without animals (cleaner environment).

There are also studies showing lung scarring after years of using chemical cleaning products. Do not scour your lungs clean. Strong ammonia or bleach-based products tend to be the worst. Use soap or gentle cleaners whenever possible and do not worry over every little spot.

57. Don't Kill The Bugs That Feed You.

If the last point did not sink it, stop trying to kill every microbe in your house or on your body. Forget the antimicrobial products. Use good old-fashioned soap. It does the job without wiping out all the healthy microbes. If you blast away all the microbes, you leave an open space to be filled. And it will be filled with opportunistic invaders that are not as friendly as the good bugs you wiped out.

58. Slash Screen Time.

There is enough evidence of potential harm with high screen use to make a serious effort to limit it. Time in front of phones, computers, televisions, handheld electronics, etc. has been linked to poor posture, degrading eyesight, interference with sleep, and negative effects on developing brains especially.

More time and research will clarify these issues over the next few years while we live in a human experiment of ever-increasing screens. Kids are more vulnerable, but we should all work on spending less time staring at screens. And consider avoiding holding a cell phone near your head. How much time is too much with screens or phones? We do not know yet, but it is worth being cautious until we do.

59. Lavatory Not Laboratory.

The bathroom has become a toxic environment in our quest for beauty and hygiene. Have you looked at all the unpronounceable chemical ingredients in soaps and washes, shampoos, conditioners, hair sprays or gels, deodorants, perfumes and body sprays, shaving products, lotions, and makeup? Your body is absorbing or inhaling (in the case of sprays) those ingredients daily. Leave the chemicals in the laboratory. Keep your lavatory clean with smarter chemical-free choices.

60. Surround Yourself With Health.

Surround yourself with healthy foods. Surround yourself with healthy activities. Surround yourself with healthy people. Surround yourself with healthy spaces.

There are people, places, and things that make the rules we have covered easier to follow. There are also people, places, and things that make it much harder to follow these tips. Surround yourself with the good stuff.

Spend time with the friend that wants to walk through nature and talk about fun stuff rather than the friend that has the worst day everyday and wants you to share their misery over a fast food meal.

Take a path to work that is prettier, makes you feel like getting active outside, and does not stress you with traffic instead of the path that has you staring at concrete walls in thick traffic driving by tempting fast food options.

Spend more time in health-promoting environments and improve the health of environments you spend the most time in.

61. Make Healthier Choices Easier To Make.

We are all lazy at times. We are programmed to conserve energy when possible. Realize this and work around it to make better choices.

You are hungry. If there is a bowl of candy in front of you and an apple down the hall, which do you choose to eat? Now there is an apple in front of you and candy down the hall in a vending machine. Which do you eat in this scenario?

Make the better choice easier to make and it is the one you will choose more often.

62. Enjoy Others.

We are social animals. We need others and they need us. Spend time with family and friends regularly. Make it a priority. Incorporate one of the other health tips at the same time for bonus points and more health benefits.

63. Work Your Brain.

Just as important as exercising your body is exercising your brain. This can be done in many ways. Do what you enjoy and then challenge yourself to try other new activities. Solve puzzles or problems, philosophize, play a new sport, learn new skills, read a variety of books. The options are endless. Keep your mind growing and expanding with new ideas, opportunities, and challenges.

64. Believe And Belong.

A study of high concentration regions of centenarians around the world noted belonging to a faith-based group was a common theme among those living to be 100 years old. Regular attendance of faith-based services increased life expectancy by 4-14 years.

TAKE ACTION

NEXT STEPS TO MAKE IT WORK

Congratulations on following some of these rules already! What can you do next? Take on the easy ones and work your way toward the bigger challenges. Here are other helpful suggestions:

1. **Set a plan** – maybe your plan is to focus on a new rule each week. Maybe your plan is to focus on a section each month. Maybe the fun ones are first. The details do not matter as much as the fact you have a plan to achieve. So set it and get it!
2. **Go big** – if you have any doubt about whether these rules effect your health, then follow as many as you can as quickly as you can. Go all in. Your body may not know what hit it for the first day or two, but within a few days (yes days not weeks) you will see changes in your health. Incremental lifestyle changes for gradual improvement are not enough for the doubters. You need big changes overnight to prove how much you control your own health.
3. **Make it a game** – call it a 30-day challenge and then get to work. Reward yourself with healthy prizes that help it stick as you make progress.
4. **Read the book again** – and again and again. Become so familiar with the rules that they pop into your head throughout the day and help guide your decisions.

5. **Inventory your hurdles** – what keeps you from following these rules? Now what can you do to get past them? Think people, places, things. Maybe someone you know needs to read the book too.
6. **Find your motivation** – is it living longer and feeling better? Is it your kids or grandkids? Find your motivation and let it drive you.
7. **Encourage yourself** – you can make great changes in your lifestyle and health. Now tell yourself you can do it. Tell yourself why you will do it and tell yourself how you will do it.

Live long and healthy!

ABOUT THE AUTHOR

Aaron McMichael, DC

Dr. Aaron McMichael is a Doctor of Chiropractic practicing at McMichael Chiropractic Clinic in Canton, Ohio with his parents and brother, helping patients improve their health with conservative care and lifestyle changes. He enjoys helping patients that have failed to find improvement with conventional medical interventions and helping patients that want to avoid medical interventions from the start. Part of the mission at the clinic is to educate, and one of the most important lessons to share is the body's ability to heal when we remove the obstacles of a poor lifestyle and support it with healthy choices.

Dr. McMichael graduated from Logan University with a Doctor of Chiropractic degree in 2007 after completing a degree in Human Biology and graduating with a degree in Biology at Case Western Reserve University in Cleveland, Ohio. While attending Logan University, Dr. McMichael interned at Jefferson Barracks Veteran Hospital, where he learned a lot from the opportunity to treat veterans with varying conditions.

Dr. McMichael has served in a variety of professional and volunteer roles including District Director and Speaker of the Board for the Ohio State Chiropractic Association, President of the North Central Academy of Chiropractic, and scout leader for Cubscout Pack 4 and Troop 4 in Canton, Ohio.

Dr. McMichael enjoys spending time, especially outdoors, with his wife Meghan and children Simon, Oscar, Elizabeth, and Philip. They are a great example of living healthy lives without the need for medical interventions.

Made in the USA
Columbia, SC
30 May 2025

58537910R00087